Thank You, Father

by William Nesmith

Thomas Nelson, Inc., Publishers.
Nashville New York

 Published by Thomas Nelson, Inc., Publishers. Nashville, Tennessee. Manufactured in United States of America.

Library of Congress Cataloging in Publication Data

Nesmith, William, 1948–
Thank you, father.

1. Fathers. I. Title.
HQ756.N48 301.42′7 76–7603
ISBN 0–8407–4047–6

To the greatest father in the world

Contents

Thank You, Father

ONE

Father, I Thank You

This morning I thought of myself as several persons.

Split personality?

I'm a fugitive from the happy farm?

No, it is simply that no one can express appreciation to a father in any single way. Fathers come in all sizes, shapes, and patterns. To say "thank you, Father" one must speak both as son and daughter, child and adult.

So, let me give it a try.

Let's take Father's Day gifts.

Let's take the pocketknife.

I was with a family at the opening of Father's Day presents. I knew what the son's present was going to be, a pocket-knife. I wondered what the look on the father's face would be when he opened that present.

Father's Day Presents

Everyone knows what the scene is like. Father sits at the head of the table looking a little embarrassed by all the attention. There is a certain sense of suppressed excitement. Then the cake is brought in, and it is time to sing "Happy Father's Day, Father" (more or less to the tune of "Happy Birthday").

In this case the cake had been decorated by one of the daughters. A work of art? Maybe.

Heavy with icing.

Yellow, because this father liked yellow.

Scalloped on the side.

"Father" spelled out in red icing on the top.

Then came the presents for Father to open while everyone else ate cake. There is always something magic about the appearance of such presents. They seem to be suddenly produced from nowhere. Oddly, this seems to bring back that magic sense of wonder and surprise that a child finds in the world.

The Happiness of Childhood

I watched the father at the head of the table. I saw the enjoyment building in his face. Imperceptibly, he seemed to change. It was like seeing him growing back in time to a happy childhood moment that itself was forever timeless.

He opened the presents. There was the inevitable shirt. The inevitable tie. The shaving lotion. The other usual Father's Day presents. He enjoyed every minute of it. So did the family.

By coincidence, my friend's present was the last one opened.

I watched the expression on the face of the father.

He looked across the table at his son.

Silence.

A Time of Insight

There is in modern literature a fascinating word, "epiphany." It describes a moment when commonplace, ordinary things suddenly reveal tremendous insight. It is a magical moment of surprisingly deep understanding. It is a moment when some great truth is at the tips of our minds, hidden but not revealed. This was such a moment.

The present was just a simple pocketknife, the kind a boy might have carried. It may even have been identical to one this same father had given this same son some long ago birthday or Christmas. And yet . . .

The look in the father's face and the returning response from his son's eyes spoke of a bond between the two that no one can put into words, least of all I. The choice of the gift showed that the son understood something about his father that few philosophers would dare to consider. Across the few feet of silent space between them there was a momentary blending of their lives. For one small timeless instant they were one. The years that separated them, the different experiences they had known, the distinction between father and son—these no longer mattered. To an outside observer like me, the father could have been the son, the son could have been the father. I suddenly realized that, for this time and this place, the son had used a small, ordinary, commonplace gift to say something profound. He was saying that he understood his father's life—not just in terms of the present but in a total way—from boyhood through old age. He understood, and he approved, and he loved his father. Symbolically, he was saying that he not only understood his father, he understood himself, and there was a common ground between them.

Journey of Understanding

All this over a simple pocketknife?

Well . . .

Yes.

There are more mysterious and profound truths in the simple things of life than there are in the momentous ones. When we start out to thank our fathers, we discover that we are on this threefold path: the understanding of fathers, the understanding of ourselves, the recognition of a common ground between child and parent.

It is the same for each of us, son or daughter.

It is a wonderful journey of understanding.

TWO

To a Yankee Father

He is alone in the skiff, and he is rowing it to the outer harbor. There is a strong southerly blowing, and there is more than a little chop on the water. A man from Indiana might find the going unpleasant, but this man is from Maine, and he is at home with the sea. He rows with strong, short strokes through the heavy waves, and the manner of his rowing tells a great deal about the man.

Maine is not a particularly gentle land. In the popular mind, it is the antithesis of Tahiti—or some other languid isle of the southern seas. In the popular mind, the man in the rowboat is a fitting symbol for this Yankee state. There is a Yankee quality of integrity which is a universal quality. The world over, one thinks of a New Englander as a man of few words —strong, sturdy, quite stubborn in holding to what he considers right. The very attitude of this man in the rowboat is symbolic of that sturdy integrity. His strokes on the oars are short but strong. He is the master of his environment.

A Strength of Fathers

What does this have to do with being a father?

I am using such a Yankee as an example of a fundamental characteristic. Integrity is not limited to Maine. There are other rocky coasts in the world. There are other hardy lands. Maine, New Hampshire, and Vermont have no monopoly on a rugged though beautiful countryside that has demanded hard work, perseverance, and courage from those who mastered it. If you don't believe me, visit Scotland (from whence came some of my ancestors).

Nor does a man necessarily have to live

in an environment that demands his development as a strong character. Don't misunderstand me. A father in Tahiti can have (and usually does have) as strong a character as a father in Toronto. A father on a lazy July afternoon in Carthage, Mississippi, is as strong a figure as a father under the gray November skies of Camden, Maine. I am using the visual image for effect, to point out a universal truth about fathers. This man in the rowboat, upright and strong, is a dramatic symbol of one of those truths about fathers we all know but seldom put into words—much less into visual symbols. Symbol is apt. No matter where one lives in the world, this figure of the Yankee carries with it certain connotations.

The New England Contribution

The person who wants to understand some of the best elements of Western culture should study New England. The pessimist who underestimates the capacity of America to continue as the leading nation of this world should study New England. The thoughtful observer who still has faith in man should study New England.

It's not just a matter of the man in the rowboat. It's not just a matter of the popular stereotype of the residents of New Hampshire—no more words in a conversation than are absolutely necessary. It's not just a matter of Yankee thrift and Yankee craftsmanship and Yankee integrity. It's not just a matter of the Puritan ethic —as modified in Maine and elsewhere Down East—of dogged hard work and self-reliant individualism.

Take this father in the rowboat. Follow him through the normal affairs of his life.

Common Sense and Ingenuity

If he lives in a typical New England small town —and some of the best small towns in the world are in New England—the commonplace details of his community life can be among the more satisfying on this planet. He belongs. He knows his neighbors. He controls his government. He takes part. He knows the selectmen. He knows what goes on at town meeting. It's his town, and he's proud of it.

Oh, the ordinary life of a small New England town may not sound like a big deal to an outsider. A New Orleans father may not see the triumph in the action of a Maine town manager who not only saves the town money by using more sand and less salt for ice control on its roadway but also improves the ecological situation by doing so. After all there is seldom glare ice on the bridge over Lake Pontchatrain. Ice control in the French Quarter usually means something other than the surface of the streets. But, in Maine, such a sensible, pragmatic, down-to-earth approach is symbolic of the Yankee way of doing things. It is a matter of using common sense and ingenuity in the small things of life so that the big things always stay real and sensible. And, after all, isn't most of life made up of the small things?

A father from Florida might feel strange at the dedication of a new chair lift in a New England town. After all, skiing means water skiing in Florida. But he would notice that the ribbon cutting was done sensibly with a pair of long shears, and he would feel at home with the dedicatory remarks of whoever represented the board of selectmen. The truth of the matter is that, when one looks at the life of a New England town, one sees the same concerns for the good life that one knows in his own community. The only thing is that, since the superficial details are sometimes different, there is sometimes a clearer perspective.

You ask: why do you talk about New England? What does New England have to do with Father?

Back to the man in the rowboat.

"Yankee"—a Universal Quality

I salute the "Yankee" in every father—I salute the concept of rugged, self-reliant individualism, of personal integrity and strength. "Yankee" stands for a universal quality that we expect to find—and usually do—in every father.

(Err . . . one disclaimer. New England people are not entirely just like everyone else in the world. Only in Maine would some of the residents upon approach of the biggest storm of the season gather at the landing at high tide to see whose wharf was going to be under water. Only in Maine would there be disappointment because the gusts of wind reached only 75 miles per hour rather than the 100 reported elsewhere on the coast. But then, if New Englanders weren't just a little different, they wouldn't be New Englanders.)

THREE

To a Southern Father

There are myths in any society that become part of the common folklore of all people. Given time, the legends pile up, reality recedes into the past, and the myth becomes larger than life and becomes symbolic of some universal attribute of all human beings. Such is the myth of "the Southerner" in American life. Let's salute a Southern father.

Perhaps no one has pictured the Southern legend in more striking terms than the novelist William Faulkner. His often quoted statement is that for the true Southerner time stops eternally that July afternoon in 1863 at the very moment when the magnificent Pickett and his cavalry stood poised in the Pennsylvania sunlight, flags flying, proud and confident, at the very instant when the War for Southern Independence reached its highest momentum. For the Southerner, says Faulkner, it is forever July, 1863. A Southerner's battle has not been lost. It is all a golden afternoon of victory, and the night is not ahead.

Southern Romanticism

Now, whether Faulkner is right or not is immaterial. Whether such a romantic concept is in the minds of contemporary Southerners is more than highly doubtful—if you insist on being realistic. The point is, the Southern legend is not based on realism. It is an expression of pure romance—romance that is, in the sense of high adventure and impossible deeds. Lost causes have a history of begetting legends. Consider Bonnie Prince Charlie in the tight little isle. But that is the point. The American South is known not only in the United States but worldwide in terms of its romantic myths.

Men Love Myths

So, what does this have to do with fathers?

Well, men love myths. And, yes, the Southern myth is an appealing one.

But let's look at the mythical Southerner.

He is a romantic figure. He almost pulled it off. The "War for Southern Independence" almost succeeded. The Southern "Cavaliers" almost defeated the federal "Roundheads." The Bonnie Blue Flag almost made it to equal status with the Stars and Stripes. So the legend arose (as legends often arise), out of the fantasy wish of persons to see things not as they are but as one might wish them to be.

Pride and Honor

If the South had won, thinks the romanticist, perhaps the modern industrial world with its impersonal, machine-dominated, technological tyranny of men would never have arisen. Instead, we might have had the indolent, comfortable, easy-going way of life the romanticist thinks existed in the antebellum South. (But that such a way of life did not in reality exist is beside the point; romance is seldom a slave to reality.)

The Southern myth is one in which a man is very much of an individual. His individual honor and his individual pride are priceless possessions to be guarded to the death. Yet his individualism is one that exists within a tight code. William Faulkner, in his acceptance for the Nobel Prize, spoke of certain human verities, of certain universal values that man needed in order to prevail. Faulkner listed his values as courage, honor, hope, pride, compassion, pity, sacrifice. He called these abstract qualities of man the glory of man's past. Now, Faulkner was a Southerner, and his own concept of human values was very heavily influenced by the fact that he *was* a Southerner. And, of course, he acted on his own assumptions. Consider the fact that he enlisted in the Royal Canadian Air Force in an attempt to fight in France before the entry of America in World War I. Southerners have no monopoly on the eternal verities, but Southerners do have a very strong claim to the romantic myth that they honor the code.

The key word is "honor."

In the Southern myth, a man's honor is his most priceless possession. This is why we salute Southern fathers. It is by singling out and emphasizing this insistence upon honor. No culture can endure without a reliance upon personal honor. Southern fathers who have taught their sons honor have done a great service.

Now, one nit-picking moment.

What About New England Integrity?

If you are very astute, you will notice immediately that there is very little difference between the Southern honor and the New England integrity. In fact, you would probably point out to me that neither New Englanders nor Southerners have exclusive rights to this cardinal quality of character.

Right.

I am merely using the Southern myth to call attention to that cardinal quality that exists in fathers everywhere, Nashville to Nairobi, Birmingham to Bangkok, Atlanta to Athens. It is that inner treasure of character I want to salute in all fathers.

There are some other things I could say about Southerners.

If you have ever known a family in a small town in the South, if you have ever attended a "family reunion," you will know how much the Southerner cares about his "kinfolks." True, concern for family exists in many other places, too. But . . .

If you have ever gone "coon hunting" with a Southern father . . .

Or spent a lazy summer in the pleasant South . . .

Maybe it would have been a happier world if the cavaliers had won. Maybe we should turn the world back to July 3, 1863.

(One explanatory note about my calling it "the Southern myth." I mean no disrespect to a lovely section of the country. My own father had the best of both worlds: his father was a Yankee, his mother a Southerner.)

To a City Father

He comes home in the evening, the modern-day equivalent of those "knights in shining armor" who used to hold their board meetings around King Arthur's Round Table. He has been jousting in the corporate tournaments all day long—or perchance slaying mercantile dragons, or mayhap rescuing companies in distress. In any event, he has been making progress in the search for the corporate Grail—else how could he afford a castle in the suburbs?

He is a city father.

(Don't worry. We'll get to the squires and pages, serfs and others, in a minute.)

Fathers—Knights in Armor?

America has worshipped so long at the altar of success that it has become traditional to satirize the man who "has it made." And, obviously, the commuting executive has it made. It is no longer a matter of Darien, Connecticut: he could just as easily have gotten off an expressway in Chicago, Atlanta, Houston, or elsewhere. He is the knight in slightly tarnished armor, riding a four-wheel steed caparisoned in plastic. By the perverse logic of the day, it is fashionable to satirize him. In fact, he probably expects to be satirized.

But . . . I wonder . . .

The Price of Success

Fathers do not cease to be fathers just because they are successful. Besides, I wonder what the human price for that success is. I suspect that the successful father from the city, commuting home to his family in the suburbs, sometimes thinks thoughts I would not want to know about. I suspect that things do not always go right at the company. I suspect there are many evenings when the miles from the city to the suburb are long and bitter. I suspect that, were it not for the family, there are many times when the successful father would chuck it all.

How much personal satisfaction can a man have in business *when things do not go right*? How does a man feel when deals that have been patiently worked out fall through? Or when bosses act arbitrarily as bosses often do? Or when the cruel infighting that is the hallmark of modern business practice leave its scars? No work is easy in this world, but the man who deals with a tangible task can at least see the actual fruits of his labor. The farmer on a tractor knows when he has plowed a good furrow. Nothing can take away from his satisfaction of having done well. He can see the result. But the man who deals in intangibles . . .

So I salute successful fathers from the city.

But with a certain wry though sympathetic irony.

The Most Wonderful Father in the World

I doubt if his children love him so much for the money he brings home, the memberships in the country clubs, or the other material things of life. I think they love him for what he is—the most wonderful father in the world. Because that is what any father is to any child—the most wonderful father in the world.

Still . . .

This one is a special case. I started out to understand fathers, all kinds of fathers. But understanding always brings with it an emotional sympathy. One learns that knights in tarnished armor really are knights. "Up guerdon! I salute thee, Sir Knight!"

But there are many other fathers in the city. Only a few make the daily pilgrimage from the suburbs. I salute the father who works all day at a dull and unsatisfying job, working to provide for his family. I salute the fathers who do dangerous but necessary jobs—policemen for instance.

Fathers Communicate Love for the City

But there's another type of father in the city. Cities have been maligned. There are historical times when it is fashionable to find fault with everything, and we live in one such time. So-called experts tell us how bad our cities are. Few persons sing the praises of the city. Yet, from the dawn of history, the city has made a tremendous contribution to human life. Cities have been centers of civilization. Despite their modern detractors, they are still wonderful places—if you happen to see the city through the eyes of a person who loves the city.

New York City, for instance, is one of the most interesting places on earth. A true New Yorker would live nowhere else on this planet. He has a lot going for his argument. It's not just a matter of all those tall buildings and the enormous amount of real estate covered by them. It's an attitude and a way of life. A New York father who loves his city communicates the reasons for his love to his own children. (He probably got it from his own father.)

The same is true in a different way of Chicago, one of the most dynamic cities on the American continent.

And then there is Los Angeles, the city that doesn't feel like a city.

I salute the fathers from the cities who love the city and pass on to their children a way of looking at the community around them.

FIVE

To a Minority Father

He was shopping in the local Sears Roebuck store, and he had his young son with him, leading the boy by the hand. He was a tall, handsome man with the confidence of success and happiness, and he was dressed as one might assume the typical executive would be dressed.

He was also a member of one of the so called minority groups.

I saw him suddenly smile, reach down and pick up his son, and kiss the boy on the cheek. Then he ruffled the child's hair and laughed and set him down again. It was such a happy, impulsive, *human* gesture that I felt good just looking at the two of them.

Why do I mention him?

Dreams and Aspirations

Well, I want to salute the minority fathers. I want to salute those like the one I saw who are in the upper mainstream of this country's culture. I want to salute those who have made it, sometimes against adversity. I want to salute the happy, successful fathers. In a sense this is unnecessary. Such persons are so much a normal part of the country's life that it seems superfluous to single them out from others.

America and the other great plural democracies succeeded because of the equality of opportunity. Yet, all societies are made up of human beings. The world is not an assembly line, and the persons in it do not move automatically down some theoretical conveyor belt to some preconceived, computer-generated destiny. Societies are living and dymanic. One of the glories of the fathers of this world is that it is up to each one individually to lead his children to cope with the particular society at hand. The dreams and aspirations of fathers are often implemented as much in the children—sometimes more so—as in the father's life itself.

Looking at this father in the store, I wonder what his own dreams and aspirations are. I wonder what his dreams and aspirations for his son are. Somehow I believe most of them will come true. He is a fine example of some of those things that we consider best about fathers.

But he is in the bright sunlight of success. The happiness on his face and the happiness on his son's face are radiant expressions. They make me feel good.

Struggles to Succeed

But there is another side.

This is not the kind of world where everything goes right all the time. At the very moment I look into this father's face, there are probably other fathers with the same ethnic and cultural backgrounds in this very city whose adversities are so recent that they remember well the struggle to succeed. I salute them, too. I salute their courage and perseverance, their determination to make their dreams and aspirations (and the dreams and aspirations they hope for their sons) come true.

Courage and Integrity

Now, of course, this really isn't just a minority matter. It happens to all fathers. Being of a minority group—ethnic or cultural—is a convenient distinction, sometimes because it is a visual distinction. For that matter, one can be in the minority even without an ethnic or cultural separation. One can even be in the topmost echelon of a society and still be a minority person. Consider the two Presidents of the United States named "Adams." John Adams was one of the Founding Fathers of the Republic. He was the second President of the United States, immediately following Washington, under whom he served twice as Vice-President. His eldest son was John Quincy Adams. John Quincy Adams, son of a Founding Father, was a very much disliked President (due in large part to his own stubborn insistance upon doing what he considered right). Yet, today in the history books, he is admired for his courage and integrity. It is always difficult to be different, and it makes little difference whether the difference is a matter of intangible values or quite visible ethnic and cultural characteristics.

Heartbreak as Well as Happiness

However, there is a special poignancy in the situation of a minority father whose dreams and aspirations for his children are complicated by a factor over which he has no control. One of the special glories of fathers is that the man of strong character, often unheralded and unsung, labors so effectively to deal with all adversities. We have all come a long way in the last 100 years. I salute the fathers who have known heartbreak as well as happiness.

SIX

To a Young Father

"Daddy! Daddy!"

My nephew is four years old. He and his mother have been visiting us over the weekend while his father is away on a trip. Now my brother-in-law drives up, gets out of the car, and my young nephew dashes toward him, shouting with happy excitement. The look on his face is something to see.

I admit to being a little jealous. Not even when I took my young nephew out to the farm and showed him the new baby pigs and the big, friendly Duroc sows was there such a look of excitement on his face. Not even when I took him out kite flying in the pasture and let him hold the string to that marvelous red kite 500 feet up in the blue Tennessee sky was there such pleasure on his face. (And my nephew has a thing about kites. He collects them. Every time he comes out for a weekend the first purchase that has to be made at Mr. Holt's store is a new kite. Our downstairs hall closet has more kites stored in it than the warehouse of the nearest kite company.)

That Wonderful Father

Nothing is more wonderful to my young nephew at this moment than the sight of his father's face. He runs to his father, and he is swept up into my brother-in-law's arms.

There is answering joy on the father's face.

My brother-in-law, like me, is of the under-thirty generation. I suppose you would call us young. In any case, we have not reached the moment in life when both the high adventure and the hard work are both past. The future lies before us, to use a very banal statement. We have our hopes and our dreams. We also have all the obstacles one must overcome in order to make it in this world. I look at my brother-in-law, and I am struck by the contrast between him as a father and my own father.

There is a photograph in our family album taken of my father when he was about the same age as my brother-in-law. He is dressed in his Navy uniform, and he has the same thin, intense, confident look about him I see in my brother-in-law now. ("Thin" is only a relative word; fathers apparently gain as much weight as wisdom with the years.) I wonder if I, too, ran to my young father with such unbounded joy on my face when I was four years old. Probably yes. It's too far back in time for me to remember. But the thought of it tugs at my heart.

A Father's Responsibility

Somewhere in the back of my memory there comes to mind the phrase "the responsibility of a family." I seem to hear it echoed in my brain. I cannot place whether it comes from some forgotten sermon in a church or from an impersonal line of type in a sociology book. Ah, how little the abstract words we are saddled with reflect true reality! I watch the face of my brother-in-law. He is not burdened down with some great "responsibility of a family." He is as overjoyed with love for his son, my nephew, as the young child is with love for him.

And yet . . .

Young fathers are special cases. My own brother-in-law is very successful in the company for which he works. But I have known other young fathers who found life a much greater struggle. So I salute all young fathers whatever their situation.

Fathers—Still Self-sufficient Pioneers

My brother-in-law works for a large national firm. He lives in the suburbs of a large city and commutes each day. He does all the typical things. For example, he is currently paneling the basement recreation room in the house he has just bought. His son will grow up remembering all the hammering and sawing. When I read all the pessimistic accounts nowadays about this country losing its sense of a frontier past, I smile. We have not lost the past; we have simply changed the form of it slightly. Our fathers remembered childhood as a time when *their* fathers were the self-sufficient pioneers who could build a farmhouse, plow a field, or repair a simple industrial machine. The pessimists tell us that those days are gone forever.

I disagree. My nephew will remember his father as one who could panel rooms or fix broken toys or paint the outside of the house. It's just a shift in emphasis. My young nephew will grow up thinking that his father can do anything. So will the children of other young fathers. And they will be right. In addition, young fathers have a special advantage in this day and time. No one knows what the future holds. It may be more marvelous than anything that we can imagine. Old fathers have lived through the wonders of the past and present. Young fathers have only the unknown and probably glorious future.

SEVEN

To an Old Father

I met him in Canada.

I met him in Florida.

I met him in Ohio.

No, not the same person. And, no, not my own father. The man I am trying to describe is someone each of us has seen many times in many places. Sometimes he is a tall, distinguished, white-haired old gentleman who carries his years with pride and contentment. Sometimes he is a frail wisp of a man. Most of the time, if we catch an unguarded view of his eyes, we get the impression that he is looking back across many years into the past, into a life already lived. Sometimes we see him on the quiet edge of the family group, an actor in a play whose center stage has moved from where he was. Sometimes we see him as the one to whom the grandchildren come because an old man seems to understand children better than the other "grownups" do.

Hands Tell a Story

There are some things about old fathers. Have you ever noticed an old father's hands? Holding a treasured Bible, long fingers extended reverently against the worn leather, an old father's hand tells of years of work and living. Hands tell a poignant story. When they were young, when they were strong and sturdy, they held the tools of work. Perhaps this father's hands once knew the warm, worn wood of an ash plow handle on a farm. Perhaps they were deft, competent hands carefully adjusting the controls of a lathe in some Midwestern factory. Perhaps they were salt-strong hands of a Cape Cod fisherman. Perhaps they once held a peavey on the Columbia River in Washington. Perhaps they were the quick, agile hands of a Texas cowboy—or the wind-toughened hands of a Montana sheepherder.

Hands tell many stories. There is a rather famous painting, reproductions of which often hang on office walls. It is the painting of an aged man saying grace before a meal. The hands are clasped firmly but reverently. With this particular painting, one begins to imagine what kind of life the man has led. Who are his children? What happiness has he known? What sorrow has he known?

The hands of an aged father may have spent their lifetime at some task that made this country. Perhaps they knew the violent vibration of a jackhammer and helped build the buildings and highways of this land. Perhaps, encased in leather faced gloves, they held the throttle on one of the mighty steam locomotives that laced this country together. Perhaps they were the hands of an artist, delicately painting a work of art that would bring joy to thousands. Perhaps they were a draftsman's hands, carefully preparing the plans for some new technological marvel of a machine.

I salute the hands of an aged father.

Love in a Father's Eyes

Hands tell a great deal about what a person has done. His eyes tell of what he has seen. The eyes of an old father have seen many things in the years in which he has lived. Looking into such eyes, I try to imagine the look in them when that father saw his first child. I see mirrored in them the successes and triumphs he has known across the years. And I see the tragedy and heartbreak in them, too.

But most of all I see love.

Not only the love the father has given out but the love he has received.

Memories of Shared Love

When one comes to the twilight of life, it must be a heartwarming thing to remember across the years the moments of shared love from family and children. I want my own father to remember me for the things that I have said to him that showed my love. I remember once, as a young man, walking with him along a busy street feeling particularly close to him, admiring him and loving him. I put my arm across his shoulder and I said, "Old man, I love you."

It may not have been high poetry, but I think he understood what I meant.

EIGHT

To a Faithful Father

He never had a great many of the world's goods. He worked hard all his life. He was never famous. There are no statues erected to his memory. No books were ever written about him. But both in the records they keep in those archives on the other side of the Pearly Gates and in the living hearts of the people who knew him, I am sure there is this phrase from the Good Book: "found faithful."

He was a faithful father.

Faithful to Responsibilities

Now, this is not to say that all fathers are not faithful. Yes, one of the characteristics of any father is the fact that he is faithful to his responsibilities. But there is something special about this father.

He was a tall man, lean, soft-spoken. In fact, his voice was so quiet one had to listen to hear what he had to say. Yet there was quiet authority in his voice. One thought of the myth of the strong, silent men of the American West, though he was not from that section of the country. He was from a quiet town in an obscure part of one of the American states. Most of his life was lived within a hundred mile circle of the place where he was born. In many ways he was typical of most of the persons he knew. A farmer in his early years and a worker in a rural area, he could have passed for a frontiersman, the men who opened this country to civilization. From middle life on, he lived in a small town where he faithfully served in one of those necessary but hardly dramatic capacities essential to a well-run community. He was one of the town's policemen.

Law and Order

Now, it is currently fashionable to either idolize or castigate the forces of law and order in America. The cycles come and go; at one time or another the television screens and the movie theaters are filled with sagas about policemen.

But they are always big city policemen. They shoot guns and drive fast cars and are always battling some sordid situation in the city. (Apparently most television script writers and modern day novelists think modern cities are nothing but concrete and stone jungles inhabited by degenerate beasts.)

But this policeman's life was not that dramatic. To an outsider, the life of a small town policeman must seem to be almost all boredom and dull routine. The bad things do not happen—or happen so seldom that it is always in some other town. I suppose the experts have never understood the real reason for this: in a small town everybody knows everybody else—and everything everybody else does. The big crimes do not happen because faithful men like this one keep in check the small crimes.

Be that as it may, though, this man spent many long lonely hours walking the nighttime streets of his town. He was a faithful guardian of law and order. Law and order can be just as important in the small things—probably more so—than in the big and brutal events.

Faith in God

Of course there are other policemen in other small towns. What made this man particularly distinctive was the fact that throughout his long life he was a happy and contented man. He had a deep faith in God. He had a high trust in the virtues and values of his community. A policeman during the week, an enforcer of law and order, on Sunday he was a faithful teacher of a Sunday School Class. During what time he had, he studied The Book. No great evangelist, no famous theologian ever loved the Bible any more than he.

Now what I have just said might apply to many men. You may even think that I know someone you know. But I am talking about a specific individual, and there is one further thing he did in his life that makes him absolutely unique. As I said, he was not a prosperous man. Yet not once, not twice, but three times in his life he mortgaged his own house in order to provide funds for the building of new churches in his community. So the man who was faithful to his community was also faithful to his God. I salute this faithful father as a symbol for all faithful fathers.

NINE

To a Father's Memory

Let's consider three places:

An obscure farmhouse in an American state, a place you will never visit—

A famous building in Washington, D.C.—

Your own home town.

First, let's consider Mr. Mac.

"Mr. Mac"

You will never meet "Mr. Mac"—at least in this life. Nor is it likely that you will ever visit the thousand acres of forest and field where he spent nearly all of his three quarters of a century life. You will see no monuments erected to "Mr. Mac" in the capitals of the world, nor will you read of his name in the history books. And yet, to those who knew him and loved him, the memory of "Mr. Mac" will be forever as green as Spring in the lovely but obscure countryside in which he spent his life.

For this father is a symbol. The memory of him could well stand for many another father in a similar circumstance far off the beaten path, in a hidden valley, in a sheltered cove. The thousand acres on which he spent his life just happened to be in a bend of the Harpeth River, more than a dozen miles to the nearest paved highway and therefore never visited by passers-by. Such a place has a timeless quality. It seems to have been there forever and to remain forever unchanged.

Memories of a Father

So what memories do "Mr. Mac's" children have of him?

They remember him as the kind, gentle father around whom—with Mother, of course—life revolved. They remember his quiet voice, his unfailing good nature, his strength and sturdiness in time of trouble or hardship. They remember his deep faith in God, and they remember his profound understanding of the beauty of the quiet world around them. One of the children became an artist; her first painting was of a wild deer. It was from her father that she had learned to appreciate the habits and the life of the wild animals of the forest. Other of the children became substantial members of nearby communities. It was from their father that they learned integrity and self-reliance, honesty and justice. From Mother too, of course, but in this happy home the role of parents was so naturally balanced that there was no conflict.

But, you ask, what has this to do with me? I never met "Mr. Mac."

But that's the whole point. There are multitudes of fathers just like "Mr. Mac" in this world. You never met them. I never met them. But the memory lives in the lives of their children.

Now let's consider a man who died in 1926—and his memory of his own father.

Remembering A Famous Father

His first name was Robert, and he was

the eldest child of his father. He served as Secretary of War in the cabinets of two American presidents. He spent four years as the United States Minister to Great Britain. As a business man, he was for fourteen years president of the Pullman Car Company, a well-known firm at the time, and was later Chairman of its Board of Directors. Surely, with such a history, you must know the man. But you don't, do you? Even if I give you his middle name, Todd, you would still not know him.

But you would know his father.

For this man's father was one of the most famous men in American history —Abraham Lincoln.

How do you think Robert Todd Lincoln remembered his father? How do you think he felt that May day in 1922 when the magnificent Lincoln Memorial Building was dedicated in Washington, D.C.? It was said of his father after that tragic assassination, "now he belongs to the ages." When your father belongs to the ages, what are your memories of him? Is it a good thing or a bad thing to share your memories with the world?

For most persons, though, the memory of a departed father is nearer to the circumstances of "Mr. Mac" than to that of Abraham Lincoln. So we come to our third place, your home town. Go down any block, and you will find that the memory of a departed father is still cherished in many a home. Oh, it may not be for some tremendous deed. My own father remembers his father as a dreamer who never quite got all his dreams together. Yet he had had a full and interesting life—not the least of it being a career as a championship racer of automobiles on dirt tracks. (To this day I am a little chary of riding with my father for I fear that he has inherited his father's lead foot.) And another member of my family remembers that her father was the best locomotive engineer in the section of the country where he lived. (But this was his public fame. I imagine she remembers him more for being a gentle father than for his ability at the throttle of a steam engine).

So there we are. I salute the memory of fathers who were loved while they lived—and are just as loved now that they are gone.

TEN

The Father I Might Be

Thank you, Father.

My intention when I began this book, was to say some very simple and heartfelt things that might express appreciation for a father. I soon came to the conclusion, though, that, in trying to express appreciation for a father, one becomes involved in understanding fathers. And, having once embarked upon a journey of understanding, one is surprised to discover that one begins to understand his own self. I think I know more about myself than I knew before I tried to understand my father. And, thirdly, there is always the matter that the father I knew inevitably becomes involved with the father I will become.

What kind of father would I like to be?

Back around the turn of the century there was a very popular song entitled "I Want a Girl Just Like the Girl Who Married Dear Old Dad." In those quiet and happy days before the First World War the song accurately portrayed the lighthearted feelings of many people. Yet there is a serious side. When we stop to think about it, most of us would paraphrase that song: "I Want to Be a Dad Just Like the Dad Who Loved and Cared for Me."

I would want my father's courage and integrity. I would want his sense of honor and duty. I would want to be as faithful as he. I would want his gentle understanding. I would want his love.

I would want my own children to remember me as I will one day remember him.

Thank you, Father, for being my father.

About the Author:

William Nesmith is an environmentalist for the state of Tennessee. He is a graduate of Middle Tennessee State University and holds a graduate degree from the University of Kentucky. This is his second book. He is also the author of Nelson's very successful *Congratulations, Graduate*. He has traveled widely in the United States and has collaborated with his own father on several books. William Nesmith is a pen name.